BOOK 1

Ways of looking

Nelson

Keith Dickson

Iain Poole

Brian Ward

About history

Recent developments promise to breathe new life into the history curriculum for students aged 14 and upwards. A major consequence of these advances will be the need to inject more purpose into the history taught to younger pupils. Several H.M.I. reports have been critical of primary and middle-school history, declaring it unambitious in terms of objectives, uncoordinated in planning and structure and unimaginative with regard to teaching method. RELIVING THE PAST is a carefully designed course in history which aims to correct these failings.

About perspectives

Since this series relates as closely as is thought appropriate to "what the historian does", great importance has been attached to teaching "what history is about". Each of the five course books seeks to develop perspectives or ways of looking at the past. THEY WERE THERE units are concerned with the people and events that "made history". Each of these units is designed to tell a story and, at the same time, critically examine the sources of evidence upon which that story is based. DAY TO DAY units are about the everyday life of people in the past and compare the work and leisure activities of different groups, living in a variety of environments, with everyday life today. STEPS FORWARD units are concerned with the idea of "change through time". These chapters examine some of the discoveries which have brought about changes to people's lives and also the effect that changes have had on the places where people have chosen to live.

About time and evidence

Each course book aims to familiarise pupils with the ideas, concepts and skills associated with time and evidence. For example, Book 1 reaches further back into the past than the Introductory Book, uncovering new periods of time whilst revising those periods previously covered. Emphasis has been placed throughout the series on the idea of looking for clues, and on the need to ask questions of and draw conclusions from them. Books 1 to 4 provide an analysis of the sources used, entitled HOW WE KNOW. Familiarity with time and evidence may help pupils to empathise with others and to feel they are "reliving the past".

Contents

Ways of Looking

This book is about people and how they lived in the past.
It will tell you about important things people have done, as well as the simple, everyday things.

It will tell you about ideas and actions that changed the way people lived in the past, and shaped the way we live today.

THEY WERE THERE

DAY TO DAY

STEPS FORWARD

These signs will remind you of the different ways of looking at the past.

THEY WERE THERE

DAY TO DAY

THEY WERE THERE units are about the important events in people's lives.

DAY TO DAY units are about ordinary, everyday matters.

The STEPS FORWARD units explain how and why things have changed.

These WAYS OF LOOKING will help you relive the past!

STEPS FORWARD

1. A soldier's tale

Grandma Walker has been showing Daniel, her grandson, some things that belonged to her father.

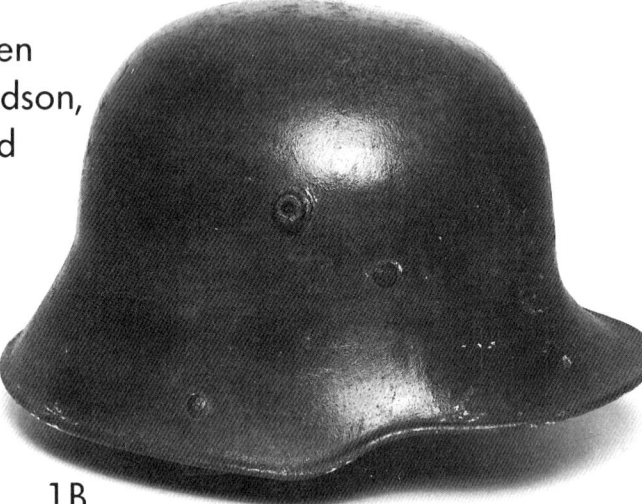

1B

1C

1A

1D

Your great-grandad was a soldier during the First World War. This photo was taken soon after he joined the army. He found this German helmet on the ground after a battle. This postcard told us he had been injured fighting in France. A piece of shrapnel like this was removed from your great-grandad's leg. This photo shows him in hospital in England. He was given this medal at the end of the war.

Can you match each item grandma spoke about with one of the pictures on these pages?

1E

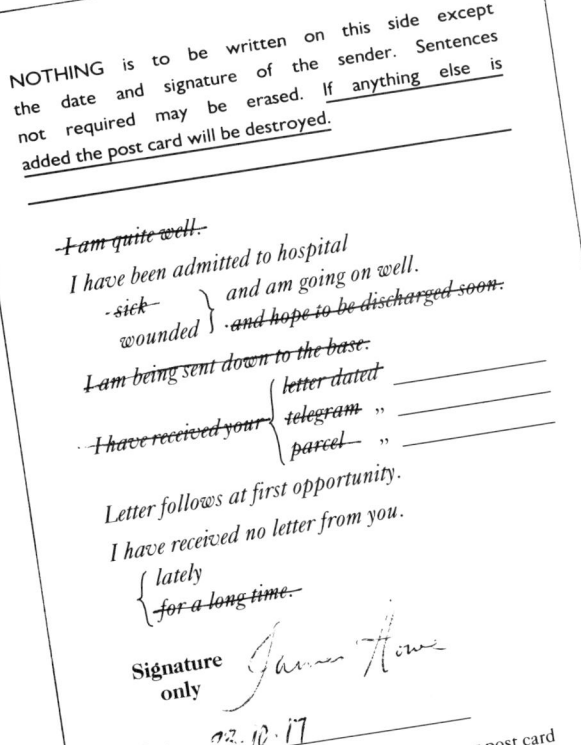

1F

NOTHING is to be written on this side except the date and signature of the sender. Sentences not required may be erased. If anything else is added the post card will be destroyed.

~~I am quite well.~~

I have been admitted to hospital

~~sick~~
wounded } and am going on well. ~~and hope to be discharged soon.~~

~~I am being sent down to the base.~~

~~I have received your~~ { ~~letter dated~~ _____
~~telegram~~ '' _____
~~parcel~~ '' _____

Letter follows at first opportunity.

I have received no letter from you.
{ lately
~~for a long time.~~

Signature only *James Howe*

Date *23.10.17*

[Postage must be prepaid on any letter or post card addressed to the sender of this card.]

Wt. W3497/293 29246. 6000m. 9/16 C. & Co., Grange Mills, S.W.

Now use the word, picture and object clues to write answers to these questions:

1. When did the First World War begin?
2. Where did much of the fighting take place?
3. What was great-grandad's name?
4. Which army did great-grandad fight against?
5. In which year was he wounded?
6. When did the war end?

The First World War was an important event in the life of Daniel's great-grandad. In this unit you will learn what happened to soldiers who were fighting alongside him.
There are word, picture and object clues which tell us "they were there".

1G

2. Joining the army

1H

James Howe joined the army soon after the war began. He was passed fit for action.
He was then sent to the south of England for training.
After this, a ship took him to France.
Later he was sent with other soldiers to the front near Ypres.
The front was where the fighting was taking place.

James passed through the towns of Southampton, Rouen, Le Havre, Leeds and Salisbury on his way to the front.
Re-write the list in the order in which he reached these towns.
Start with Leeds, which was where he joined the army.
Use clue 1H and an atlas to help you.

1I

a

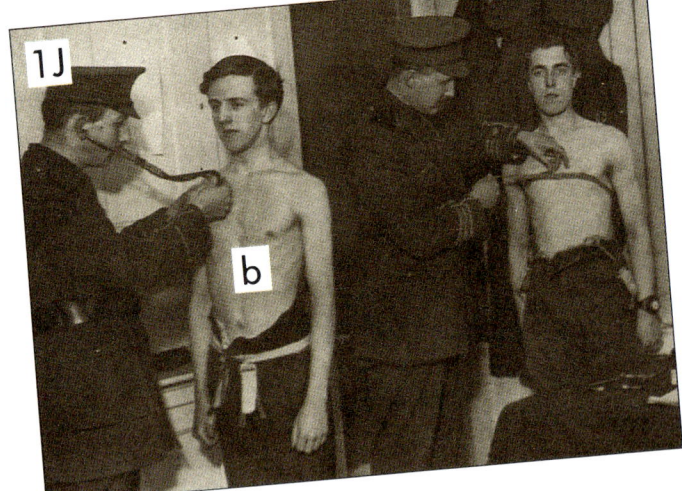

1J

b

1K

c

1 L

d

The six photographs on these pages tell us what happened to some other men who wanted to join the army when the war broke out.

Write a sentence to say what each man marked with a letter was doing at the time his photograph was taken.
The things that happened to James Howe will help you do this.

1 M

e

Here is a list of items that soldiers like (f) had carried with them to the front.

pipe and tobacco	
compass	identity disc
heavy overcoat	water bottle

Can you think of other things to add to this list?
Write down why you think each item would be needed.

1 N

f

3. The view from the front

This picture of the front was drawn during 1915.

By that time, the soldiers on each side had dug rows of deep trenches in the ground. The trench walls protected soldiers from the bullets and shells fired at them.

Which armies faced each other at this part of the front?

Look at the writing on the picture to find the answer.

How many lines of trenches can you see? The space between the trench in the foreground and the German front line was called "No Man's Land". Can you think why?

10
German second line
German front line
75 Shell
Steel Shield
crater
dead German
Shell crater

Now look at the French soldier in the bottom right hand corner of the picture. He was using an object called a periscope to look from his trench across to the lines of German trenches.

Why was a periscope useful to have in the trenches?

Imagine you were the soldier using the periscope.
Write some sentences to say what you could see:
1. between your own trench and the German front line.
2. between the lines of German trenches.
3. behind the German second line.

4. Under attack

The paintings on these pages show Canadian soldiers in the trenches. Those in 1P were facing an attack made with poison gas.
Why do you think gas was used as a weapon?
Why could it be used only when the weather was windy?

What makes you think that the soldiers in the picture were taken by surprise when the attack with gas was made?
How did they protect themselves from the deadly fumes?
Write sentences to say what three different soldiers did.

1P

Picture 1Q shows a group of Canadians defending a trench from a large number of German soldiers who were trying to capture it.

Make a list of the objects the Canadian soldiers were using to protect themselves.

Did you find these objects in the picture?

rifle   sandbag   bayonet
grenade   machine gun

Make a drawing of each object and write a sentence to say how it was used.
Which of these things was it most important for soldiers to have in the trenches?

1Q

5. Over the top

When soldiers left their trenches to attack enemy trenches it was called going "over the top".

Can you think why?

The pictures on these pages show what happened when an attack "over the top" was planned.

Imagine you were one of the soldiers taking part in this attack.
Copy and complete the sentences on page 15 about what took place. Use these pictures and the words in the box below to do this.
You may use two words more than once.

> trench bayonets writing enemy
> walls shells guns sleeping

1S

1R

"Our _____ fired _____ at _____ lines for a week before the attack.

We passed that week talking or _____ home, eating and _____ when we could.

When the _____ stopped firing, we made ready and fixed our _____.

Then we climbed the _____ _____ and set off towards the _____."

Now use your own words to say what happened next:

"We moved slowly across No Man's Land because of the _____ and _____ everywhere.

From time to time we_____ to shelter from enemy fire.

My ears were bursting with the sounds of _____.

I was wounded in the leg when_____ _____."

6. After the battle

Picture 1V shows the results of an attack by British soldiers on enemy lines.

Copy and complete the chart below about the different things that took place. Use the numbers on the painting to guide you.

EVENT NUMBER	WHAT HAPPENED
1	German shells made huge craters in the ground.
2	
3	Trees lost their branches and leaves.
4	
5	
6	Fresh soldiers advanced towards German lines.
7	
8	British guns were moved forward and more shells fired at German lines.

Which of these events most likely took place before British soldiers went over the top?

Which happened after they had gone?

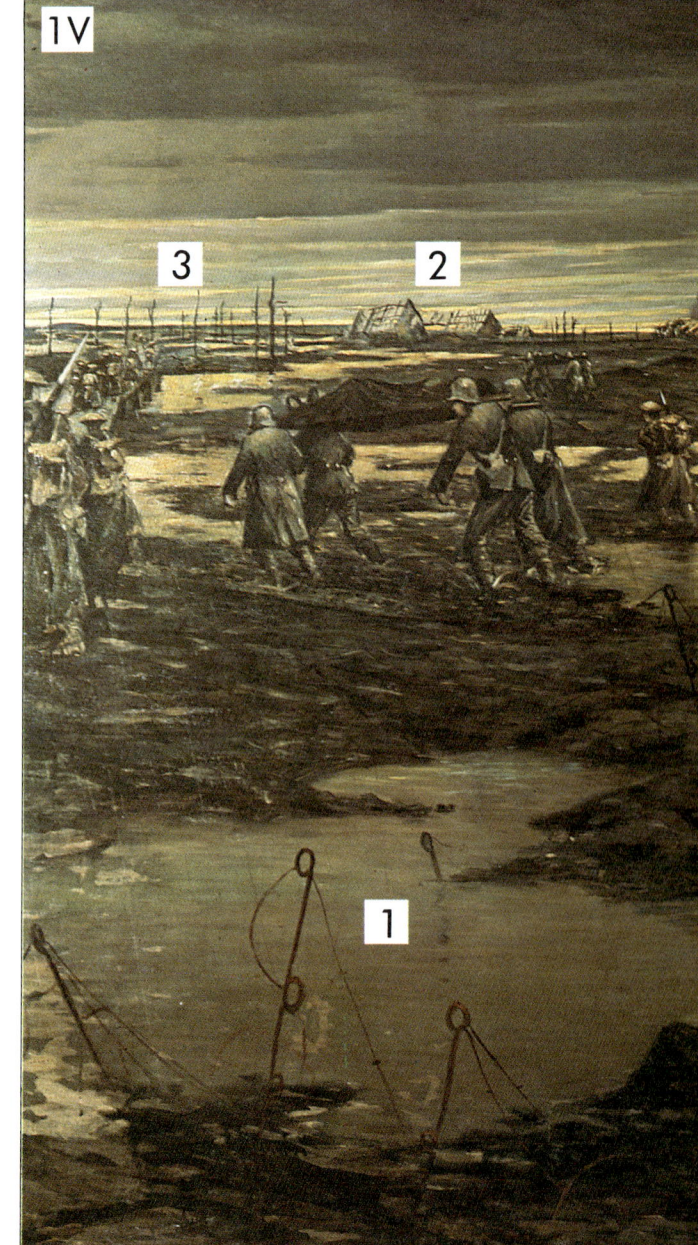

Now look more closely at the group of soldiers making their way behind British lines.

Some of these soldiers were British.

Others were German prisoners. How can you tell?

Some wounded men were stretcher cases. How many can you see?

What other injuries did different soldiers have?

How were these injured men being helped to safety?

Find out from books what happened to soldiers who were wounded at the front. Then imagine you were one of the injured soldiers in this picture.

Use these words to write sentences about what happened to you after the battle.

bandage   ship   shrapnel

dressing station   hospital

7. To take you further

This picture shows a model of a British trench which has been rebuilt at the Castle Museum, York.

Which of the different parts of a trench can you see in the picture?

How is the model trench different from the trenches shown in pictures 1Q and 1S?

Trenches were often given names, like King George Street or Death Valley. Why do you think names were used?

Make a model of a trench in your classroom.

Give your trench a name and label its different parts.

Poppies grow in the fields of Northern France, where battles of the First World War were fought.

Every year, poppies help us remember those who died.

On Poppy Day, many people visit a war memorial near their home.

Write sentences to say what these people wear and do on Poppy Day.

Where is the nearest war memorial to your home?

Draw a picture or take a photograph of it.

How many names of those killed during the First World War are recorded there?

Find out how the money people give each year for poppies is used.

UNIT TWO
AT HOME WITH THE VICTORIANS

DAY TO DAY

1. The family home

Picture 2A shows Osborne House on the Isle of Wight.
It was built as a summer home for Queen Victoria, her large family and their many servants.
Queen Victoria was the great-great-grandmother of Queen Elizabeth the Second.
But very few people lived in homes like Osborne House when Victoria was queen.

Picture 2B shows where the Fothergill family lived in the town of Leeds one hundred years ago. There were seven people in the family and they had only one room in which to live.

2A

Write some sentences to say what you like or dislike about each of these buildings.

2B

WATERLOO COURT

Now look at the houses in picture 2C. How different were these houses from Osborne House and the house where the Fothergill family lived?

The Curtis family lived in one of the houses in 2C when Victoria was queen.
Mr William Curtis had just left his home when the photograph was taken.

What was Mr Curtis about to do?
How can you tell that he was a rich and important man?

This unit is about the Curtis family, and other families like them.
There are word, picture and object clues which will tell us about their "day to day" lives.

2C

2. Who's who?

2D is a photograph of the Curtis family.
William Curtis married Jane Heath in
1830.
They had two daughters, Sarah and
Louisa; then three sons, William, Thomas
and Charles.
Sadly Thomas was drowned at sea in
1865.
Their youngest children were Maria and
Arthur.
William Curtis was a doctor.
His sons William and Arthur also became
doctors.

Photograph 2D was taken in 1866.
Try to name each person you can see in it.
Which members of the family were not in
the photograph?
Can you think why?

Have you a photograph which shows the
members of your family?
How is your photograph different from
2D?

The Curtis family had servants to do their cooking and housework, to serve meals and look after the garden.
2E shows the servants kept by another family in Victorian times.
Look for these servants in the photograph. Write down the clues which tell you what each servant did.

cook
cook's assistant
gardener
gardener's assistant
housekeeper
housemaid
coachman
odd jobs man

2E

Servants had to be well behaved. Choose one word from those in brackets to complete each of these rules for servants.

Then add some rules of your own to this list.
2E will give you ideas.

1. (Never/always) tell the truth.

2. Go about your work (quietly/noisily).

3. Never get up (late/early).

4. Always be (rude/polite) to visitors.

3. Early to rise

Picture 2F was taken at Bradford Industrial Museum.
It shows you what a bedroom in a large house was like when Victoria was queen.
Mr and Mrs Curtis's bedroom may have looked like this.

The Curtis family had these objects in the bedrooms of their house.

2G
chamber pot
towel rail
vase
wash-stand
candlestick
fender and fire irons

Find the objects in the picture and make a drawing of each.
Why do you think there was a wash-stand in a bedroom?

2F

Martha Cooper was a servant who worked for the Curtis family.
Every day servants like Martha had to get up early in the morning, in order to begin their jobs.

Write about the jobs Martha would have had to do in the bedrooms:
1. before the Curtis family went down to breakfast.
2. after breakfast had begun.
Look for clues in picture 2F to help you.

Make drawings of pieces of furniture in your bedroom to go alongside your drawings of furniture in this bedroom.
How different is your bedroom from the one in this picture?

4. During daylight hours

Servants had to work very hard to keep houses and gardens clean and tidy.

These pages show some of the objects servants used in Victorian times.

Which of these objects would servants have used to do these everyday jobs?

1. Mow the lawn.
2. Clean cutlery.
3. Warm the bed.
4. Clean out the stables.
5. Clean a carpet.
6. Make the fire.

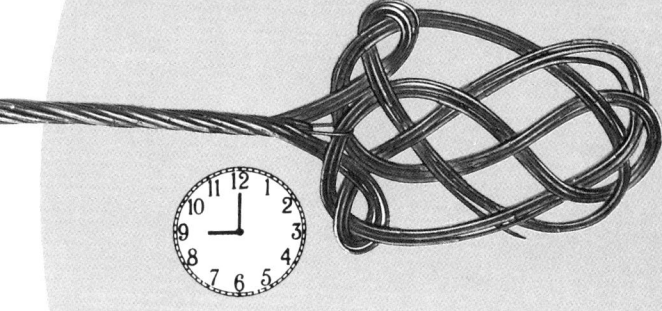

Draw up a chart to record this information:
1. What each job was.
2. A drawing of the object used to do each job.
3. The name of the servant from picture 2E who would have done each job.

JOB	OBJECT	PERSON

THEN

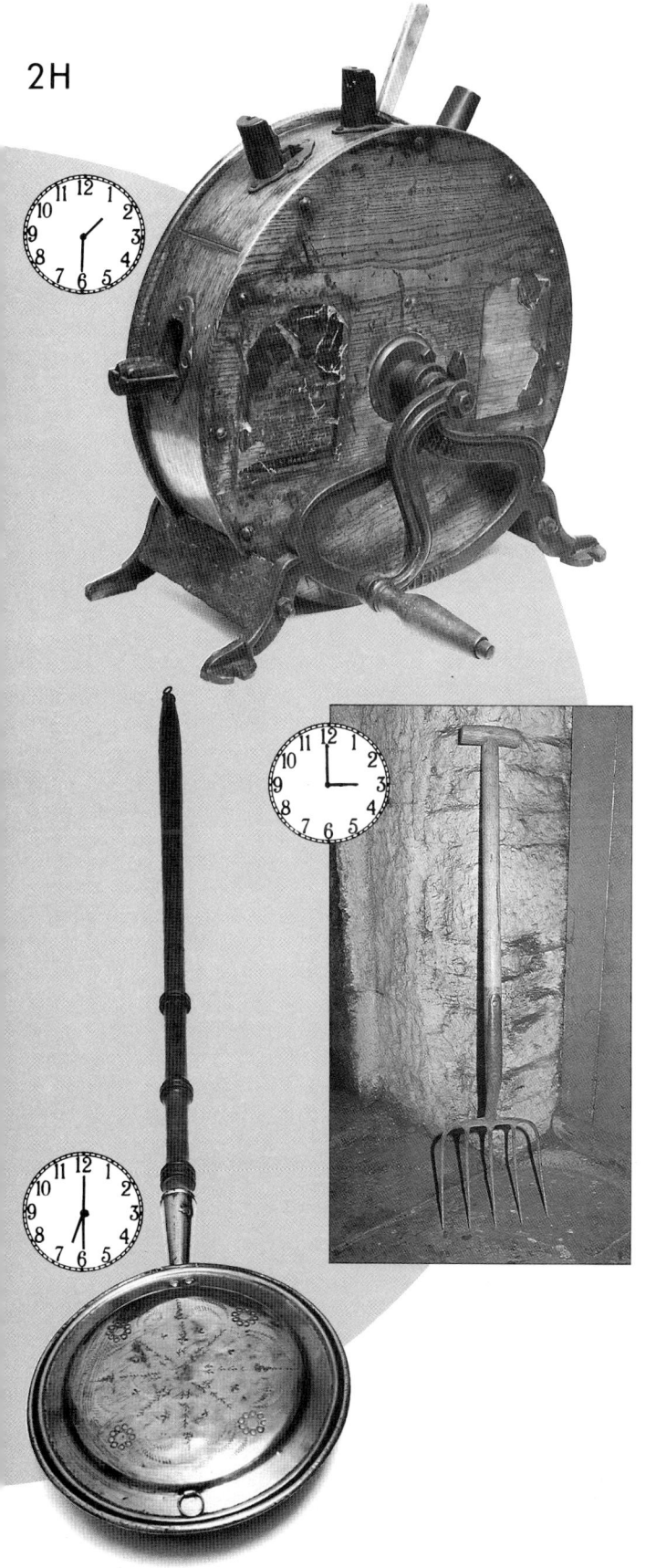

Which of the jobs in your list still need to be done today?

Sketch the objects we use to do them now.

Which people do these jobs in your home?

Draw up another chart to record this information.

JOB	OBJECT	PERSON
	NOW	

What do you imagine the members of the Curtis family were doing during daylight hours?

There are word and picture clues on page 22 that will give you ideas.

Do you think they worked as hard as their servants?

5. Evenings at home

The family this artist has painted were spending an evening at home.

The servants of the house had done many jobs to make the room ready.

These are some of the things they had done.

1. Lit the oil lamp.
2. Cleaned the tiger skin rug.
3. Watered the plants.

21

Add some more jobs to this list.
Picture 21 will give you ideas.

Now write some sentences to say what the different members of the family were doing.

Here is another list of objects owned by the Curtis family.

2J
sewing machine

writing table

cottage piano

collection of fossils and shells

oak bookcase

card table

Use the list to write about how the different members of that family might have spent an evening at home.

How do the members of your family like to spend an evening at home?

Write some sentences to set alongside what the Curtis family did.

Would you have enjoyed an evening at home in Victorian times?
Say why.

6. Guests for dinner

Mr and Mrs Curtis often had guests for dinner.
At such times, their servants had many jobs to do.

Write a sentence about a job the servants might have done:
1. in the cellar.
2. at the front door.
3. in the dining room.
4. in the bedrooms.

Now look at 2K below:

Which room can you see in the picture?
The lady of the house is talking to her butler or manservant. What do you imagine she is telling him?
What can you see the other servants doing?

2K

Picture 2L shows the dining room in a large Victorian house.
How many dinner guests can you see in the picture?
How many servants were there to help?

How is the evening meal-time in your home different from the one taking place in picture 2L?

Think about:
1. the number of people eating together.
2. how the people are dressed.
3. the amount of food eaten.
4. how the food is set out.

What do you imagine the servants did after the evening meal was over?

7. To take you further

This picture shows a dolls' house which was made when Victoria was queen.
Only a few children lived in houses like this one in Victorian times.
How many rooms did this house have?

Draw a picture like this to show how each of these rooms was used.

Can you think of a different job for a servant to do in each room?

Find out from books about the other toys children played with in Victorian times.

	Kitchen			

The picture on this page shows the inside of a house like the one the Fothergill family lived in.

How was this room different from the room in picture 21?

Find out from books about the everyday lives of poorer people in Victorian times. What would the Curtis children have owned and done that the children of the Fothergill family did not?

Many young people left homes like the one in this picture.

They became servants in houses like the one the Curtis family owned.

Would you have wanted to be a servant in a large house in Victorian times?

Think about the good points and the bad points.

UNIT THREE
CHANGES IN THE STREET

1. Old street, new street

People are always changing.
They grow taller, look older, wear different clothes.
The things around them change too.

Photograph 3A shows a street as it looked in Victorian times.
You can see from photograph 3B that this same street looks very different today.

1	A clothes shop once stood on the corner of this street.
2	
3	There were public toilets in the middle of the street.
4	
5	The Albion Hotel stood here.
6	
7	
8	

This unit is about how and why streets have changed during the last 100 years.
Write about some of the changes in this street by copying and completing the THEN and NOW chart below.

Do you think it was safer to cross the street THEN than it is NOW?

1	A McDonald's snack bar now stands on the street corner.
2	
3	
4	
5	
6	
7	
8	This modern office block has a flat roof.

2. Old rules OK?

The buildings in picture 3C are old, and have not been replaced by more modern ones. This is because a new use has been found for them.

Choose one word from those within the brackets to complete each of these sentences about the buildings:

In Victorian times, the buildings were (offices/cottages) made of (stone/brick). Then their (ground/upper) floors were converted into (flats/shops), and these rooms were extended over what had been the (front/back) gardens.

Add a further sentence to say why you think these buildings changed in use.

3C

The buildings in picture 3D were also houses in Victorian times.
This <u>street directory</u> tells you who lived there 100 years ago.

Who lived at number 279 then?
How is this building now used?
Why is the front window larger than it used to be?
What happened to the front garden?
A railing once separated this garden from the road beyond.
Draw a picture to show what you think number 279 looked like in Victorian times.

273 Winn Benjamin, milliner
275 Scott Joseph E., woollen manfr.
277 Horsfall Mrs.
279 Dickinson Anthony
281 Madden Wm. A., inland rev. officer

3D

3. Down with the old ... up with the new!

In many streets the old buildings have been pulled down to make way for new ones.
This happened some years ago to the shops you can see in this old photograph.
Why do you think this was done?

THOMAS HARGRAVE COWKEEPER

MARY E. FIELDHOUSE FENT DEALER

JOSEPH SOWDEN BLACKSMITH & CARTING AGENT

MARTIN GILL COOPER

MARK STEVENSON SADDLER

These are some of the shops you could have visited along this street 100 years ago.

Find out what each of these shops sold. Why do you not see shops like these today?

A new shopping centre has now been built on this street.
Picture 3G shows what the street looks like today.
Why were the new shops not built where the old ones had stood?

3G

MORRISONS SUPERMARKET	**Granada TV & VIDEO**	**Y E B ELECTRICITY**
Iceland Frozen Foods Ltd.		**"OPEN SEVEN DAYS" CAR PARTS 567 130**

These are some of the shops in the new shopping centre.
Which of these shops could you not have visited 100 years ago?
Why not?

Find out from books about the changes to shops and shopping that have taken place since photograph 3F was taken.
Which do you like best: old shops or new shops?

4. Changes in size and shape

When old buildings are pulled down or when new ones are built, the street changes in size and shape.

Map 3H shows a street as it was 100 years ago.

Map 3I shows the same street as it is today.

Here are the outline shapes of some buildings on these maps.

Can you work out which buildings they are?

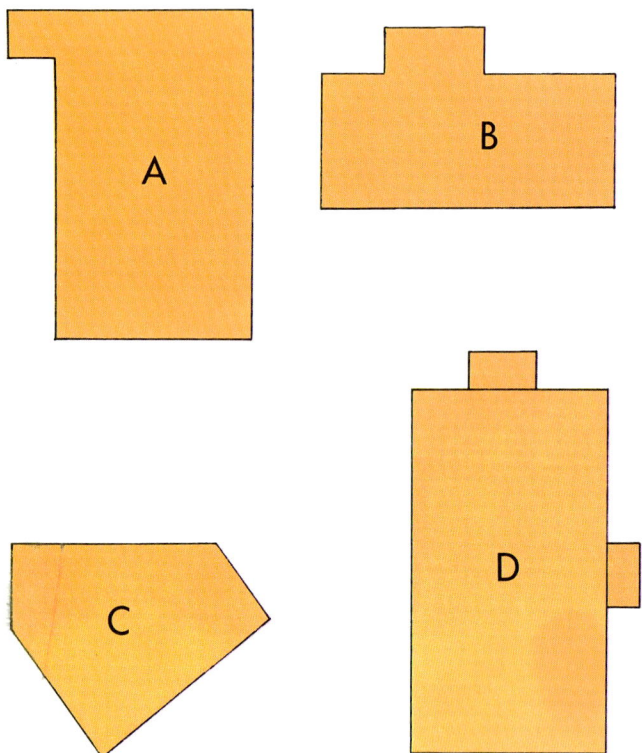

Which of these buildings have been pulled down since map 3H was drawn?

Which have been built since map 3H was drawn?

Add more buildings from the maps to these lists and draw its outline shape alongside each.

3H

= HOUSES

= SHOPS

ABBEY INN

METHODIST CHAPEL

KIRKSTALL TANNERY

MILL POND

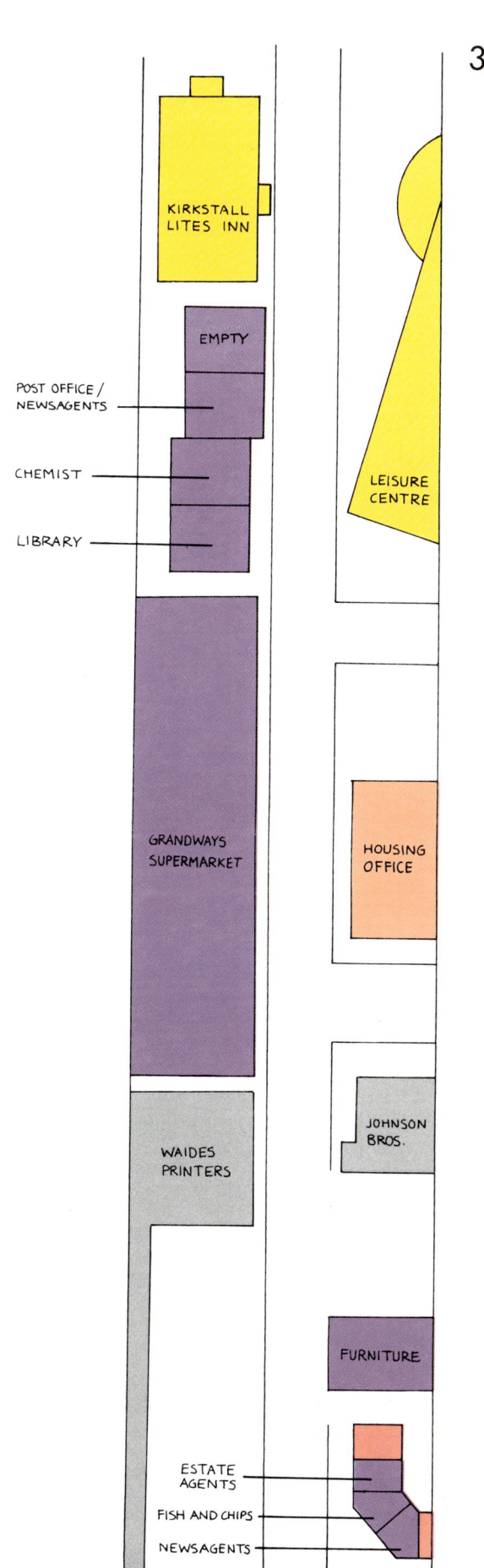

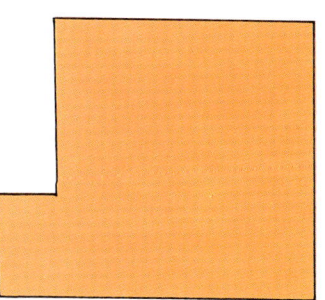

Now look for this old building on map 3H:

Can you find the same building on map 3I?

Write a sentence to say how the building has changed during the last 100 years.

Add a further sentence to say why you think this change has happened.

Find out about the changes in size and shape of a street near your school.
Show the changes in words and pictures like this.

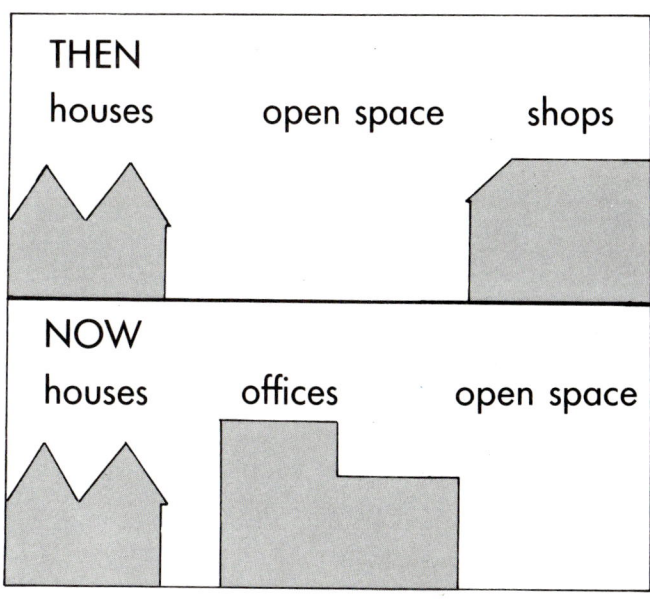

5. The street at play

Pictures 3J and 3K show children at play in the street.

Write some sentences about the games they were playing.
Are these games still played today?

Children used to play many games in the street.

Ask older people to tell you why.
Why do children not play in the street as much today?

Ask older people about the games they played when they were young.

Then choose one game played both then and now and say how it has changed.

Write about:
1. where the game was/is played.
2. how players were/are dressed.
3. the equipment that was/is used.
4. the rules of the game then/now.

3L

Street entertainers were often seen in the past.
Ask older people about the different entertainers and the animals they saw.

Imagine you were one of the children in photograph 3L.
Write about what you saw, heard and did when this entertainer came down your street.

3M

The people in picture 3M were visiting the cinema.

Why do you think cinemas were so popular in the past? Why are they less popular now?

Find out what places of entertainment there used to be in the streets near your school.

Which of these buildings have:
1. stayed the same?
2. been pulled down?
3. changed in use?

3N

Picture 3N was painted about 100 years ago.

Copy and complete the chart below about the jobs people did in the street then. Use the letters on the picture to guide you.

A	Selling oranges
B	
C	
D	Driving a bus
E	
F	
G	
H	Sweeping the road

How have these jobs changed since the time this picture was painted?

A group of three or four pupils could talk about each of the jobs.

Each group could then give a report of its discussion to the rest of the class.

Why have some of the jobs changed more than others?

Objects can provide clues about the street at work.

Can you see a milk cart in the picture? Find out how people got their milk 100 years ago.

Is the milkman's job easier now than it was then?

How many street lamps does the painting show?

Find out how lamps like these were lit in the past.
Why is this job no longer done?

Ask older people about the street at work when they were young.

Are the things they saw still being done today?

7. To take you further

The black dots on this picture mark changes to Town Square in Cluebury. The speech boxes tell you what people who live in the town think about the changes. Can you match the dots with the boxes?

What do you think about the changes? Write your own speech box for each one. You must either agree or disagree with what each person from Cluebury has said, and then explain why.

I feel safer crossing this road . . .

They should look after old buildings . . .

That will be handy . . .

That wall . . . it's ugly . . .!

What use is that?

The square is much cleaner now . . .

Can't hear myself think . . .!

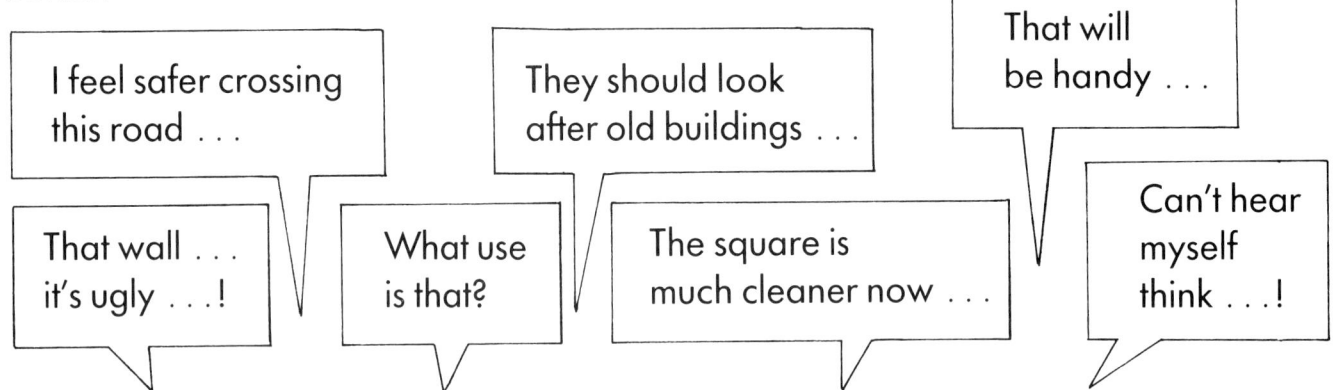

What does your class think about changes in the streets near your school?

A street named after a building or some other local landmark can help us imagine what the street looked like in the past.

These pictures show different streets in Cluebury, as they look today.
How do you think each street got its name?

STATION PLACE

OAKWOOD DRIVE

CASTLE STREET

Draw a picture to show what each street used to look like.
Then write about how each street has changed.

Look for street names like these where you live.
What do they tell you about your town or village in the past?

YEARS   1   2   3   4

A lifeline can tell you about the things that happened to a person
and when each event took place. The red line above shows the lifeline of Lisa Walker.
Use the lifeline to answer these questions:

1. Which of these events happened <u>first</u>, or <u>earliest</u> in time?

2. Which event happened <u>last</u>, or was most <u>recent</u>?

> Lisa went to school.
> Lisa's younger brother was born.
> Lisa was baptised.
> The Walkers moved house.

3. Which one of these events happened <u>before</u> the others?

4. Which event happened <u>after</u> the other events?

> Lisa broke her leg.
> The Walkers went on holiday to London.
> Lisa took her first steps.
> Lisa was a bridesmaid.

1880   1890   1900   1910

The blue line below shows the lifeline of
James Howe, who was Lisa's great-grandfather.

Using time words or numbers, copy and complete these sentences about James's lifeline:

1. James was born in _____ and died in _____ .

2. James was at work when he was _____ old.

3. Grandma Walker was born soon _____ James bought his first car.

4. James was married _____ he went to war.

Now write four more sentences about the lifeline of James Howe.

Use the time words and/or numbers on these pages in each sentence.

UNIT FOUR
AT THE TIME OF RICHARD BEAUCHAMP

1. A child is born

This unit is about a rich and important Englishman named Richard Beauchamp.
Richard was born 600 years ago.

When he died, a book was written about his life. Pictures 4A to 4H are all taken from this book.

Picture 4A shows Richard as a new-born baby.

Which event does picture 4B show taking place? How can you tell this happened some months after Richard was born?

4A

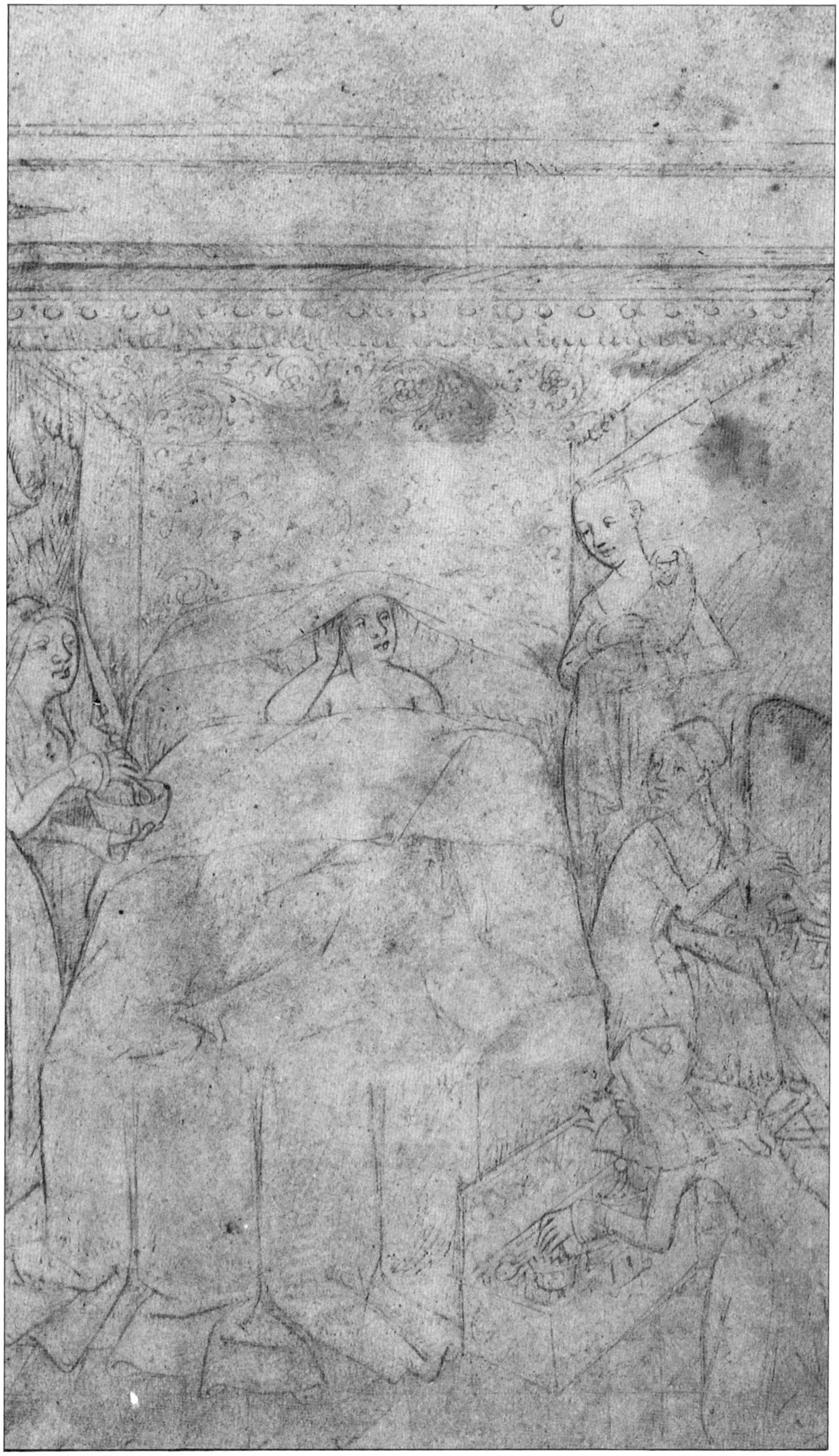

Pictures 4A and 4B show some of the important people in Richard's life.

Can you see: (a) his mother; (b) his nurse; (c) the bishop who baptised him; and his godparents (d) King Richard the Second and (e) Richard Scrope, Bishop of Lichfield?

Write a sentence to say what each of these people was doing.

Why do you think his parents called their son Richard?

Which people have been the most important in your life?

His baptism was an important event in the life of Richard Beauchamp. Make a list of the main events in your life. Then draw a lifeline to show the events in the order in which they happened.

2. Becoming a knight

Richard's book tells us that he became Earl of Warwick and the most famous knight in England.
But it does not tell us how he grew up. However, we do know about the lives of other rich boys who lived at the same time.
Most likely, Richard had to learn to:

1. read and write
2. ride a horse
3. use a sword
4. serve at table
5. hunt animals
6. be polite
7. clean armour
8. play games
9. sing and dance
10. take messages

Which of these things:
1. can you do now?
2. will you learn later?
3. are you never likely to learn?

Richard was made a knight at the age of 17.

In picture 4C, Richard kneels before the new king, Henry.

What has Henry placed around Richard's neck?

Behind the king stands the sword-bearer, and beside the sword-bearer a man who was most likely Richard's father.

Write sentences to say how Richard, his father and King Henry were dressed for this event.

Find out from books how a young man was made a knight.

What promises did he have to make?

You could then act out what happened in your classroom.

3. Fighting games

In 1403, King Henry the Fourth was married.
A great tournament was held after the new queen was crowned.
Richard was the queen's champion at this tournament.
He had to joust with every knight who challenged him.

Can you find Richard in picture 4D?
He is wearing his family crest, a bear and ragged staff, on top of his helmet.
How was this a help to the spectators?
Jousting was an exciting but dangerous sport.
What was Richard trying to do?
What had happened to his lance?
Why do you think there was a fence between Richard and his opponent?

4D

Now look at those people who were not taking part:
Which person was helping Richard? How can you tell?
Where were the king and queen seated?
What was the Master of the Joust checking?
Why were two spectators having their own battle?

Imagine you were one of the spectators at this tournament.
What did you see, hear and smell?
Here are some ideas.

dust	flags	cheers	blood
	trumpets	horses	prizes

Use the word and picture clues on these pages to add to this list.
Then use the words in some sentences.

4. At the Battle of Shrewsbury

A few months after the tournament,
Richard took part in a real battle.
He was fighting on the side of King Henry
against soldiers led by Sir Henry Percy.
In picture 4E the soldiers of the king were
drawn on the left.

Can you find Richard? What was he
doing?
Where was Sir Henry Percy? Look for his
crescent-shaped crest.
What had happened to him?
How does the picture show that Percy's
soldiers were defeated?

Make a drawing or model of a crest that
you might have worn in a battle like this.

4E

Now look at the archers and other foot soldiers who took part in the Battle of Shrewsbury.

Why were they wearing lighter armour than knights like Richard Beauchamp?

Make drawings of the different weapons that archers and foot soldiers were using in this picture.
Which weapon do you think was the most dangerous?

Would you have wanted to be a knight, archer or foot soldier in this battle?
Write some sentences to say why.

How different was a battle at the time of Richard Beauchamp to one when James Howe was a soldier?

5. At the gates of Rouen

After Henry the Fourth died, his son, also called Henry, went to war with France. 4F shows the English army outside the French town of Rouen.

Copy and complete these sentences about the picture:

Rouen was surrounded by
thick _____ and high _____.
There were _____ on the _____
ready to push back an attack.
The _____ across the _____ had
been raised.
The English were camped behind
a wooden _____.
They had brought _____ to fire at
the town.

Use the words in the box below to do this.

battlements	moat
walls	drawbridge
cannons	fence
soldiers	towers

Now use your own words to complete this sentence:

King Henry the Fifth was _____
outside his _____ giving orders to
_____ who was _____ before him.

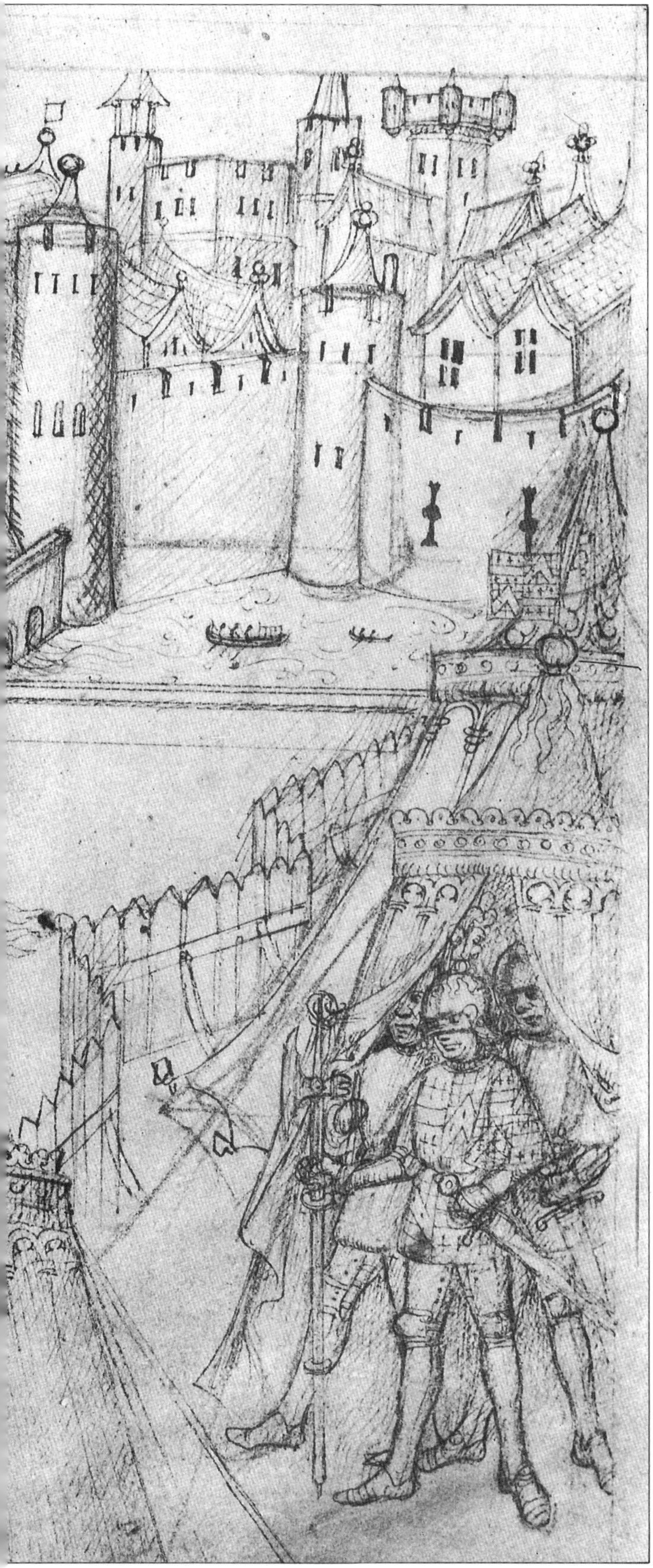

How would you have planned to capture Rouen, if you had been Richard Beauchamp?

Here are some ideas other armies used to capture towns.

1. Dig a tunnel under the wall.
2. Use a tree trunk to break down the gate.
3. Shoot fire bombs over the wall.

Use the picture to add your ideas to this list.
Think about the good points and bad points of each plan.

Then write down why you chose the plan you did.

Turn to page 95 to find out what the English army decided to do at the gates of Rouen.

6. Laid to rest

The next king, Henry the Sixth, gave Richard the job of ruling over English land in France.
It was in the town of Rouen that Richard died in 1439.

Picture 4G shows him on his death bed.

His body was returned to England and buried in a tomb in St Mary's Church, Warwick.

Picture 4H shows Richard's funeral.

Copy and complete this chart to show what each of the lettered figures in these pictures was doing.

A	was blessing the dying Earl.
B	held the oils used to do this.
C	
D	was holding the Bishop's staff.
E	
F	
G	
H	

4G

Draw a lifeline to record the important events in Richard's life.

First match these dates and events correctly.

1381	Richard died
1399	At the gates of Rouen
1403	Richard born
1418	Richard knighted
1439	Battle of Shrewsbury

Then mark each event on your lifeline. Which picture in this unit tells you about each event?

Which kings ruled England during Richard's life?
Re-read pages 51, 54, 58 and 60 to check your answers.
Find out from books when each king ruled and enter these dates on your lifeline.
Then write some BEFORE and AFTER sentences about the events you have recorded.

4H

7. To take you further

This effigy of Richard Beauchamp was made after his death.
It is a life-like figure, first carved in wood and then cast in bronze and covered with gold.

Draw an outline copy of the effigy and label these parts:

1. the jousting helmet, with the swan's head crest on top.

2. the small crown or coronet around the helmet.

3. plate armour to protect the body, arms, legs and feet.

4. the straps which held pieces of armour together.

5. chain mail worn under the plate armour.

6. Richard's sword.

7. the garter Richard wore, as a "Knight of the Garter".

8. the bear and griffin at his feet.

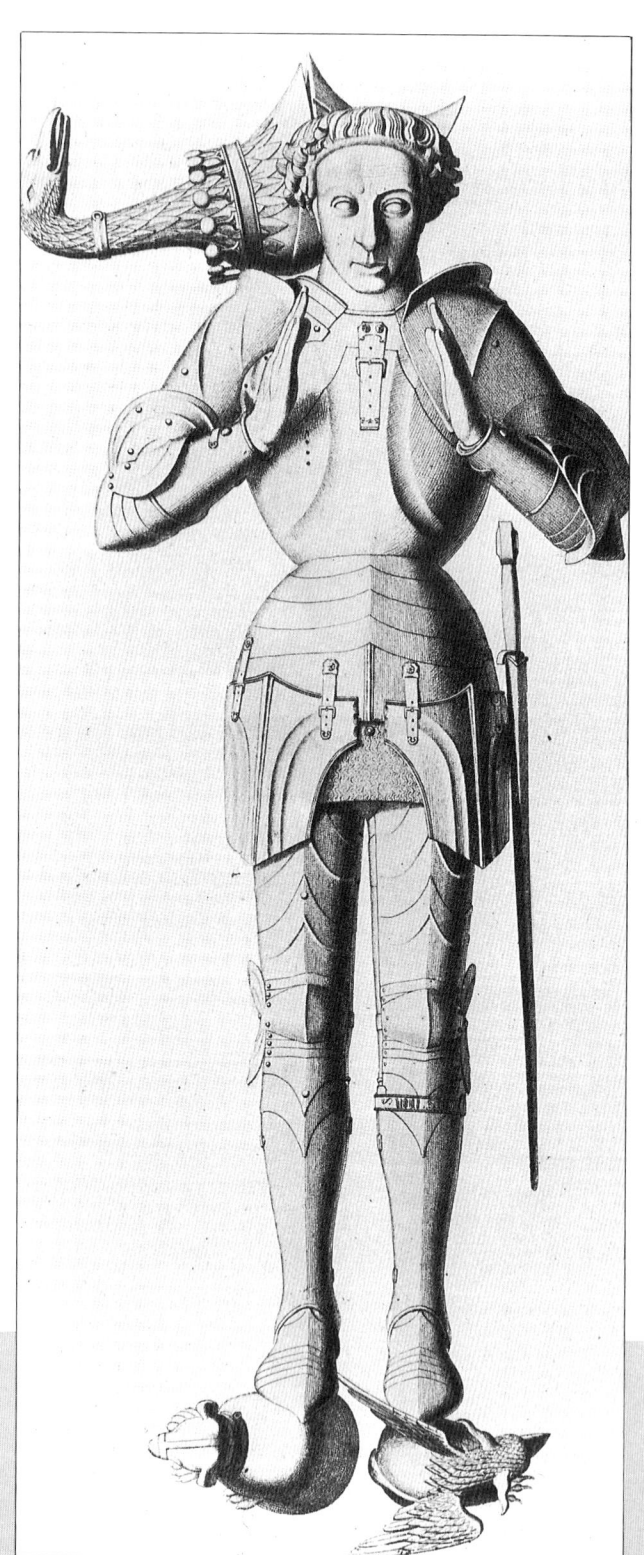

Fifteen years after he died, Richard's body was placed in this marble tomb.

Where was the effigy laid?

Around the sides of the tomb, angels and figures called "weepers" were carved. Who do you think the weepers were meant to be?

Look at tombs and gravestones in the churches and churchyards where you live.

How many of these questions can you answer about people buried there:

1. What were their names?
2. When were they born?
3. What did they look like?
4. What did they do?
5. When did they die?
6. How did they die?

What do his tomb and effigy tell you about Richard Beauchamp?

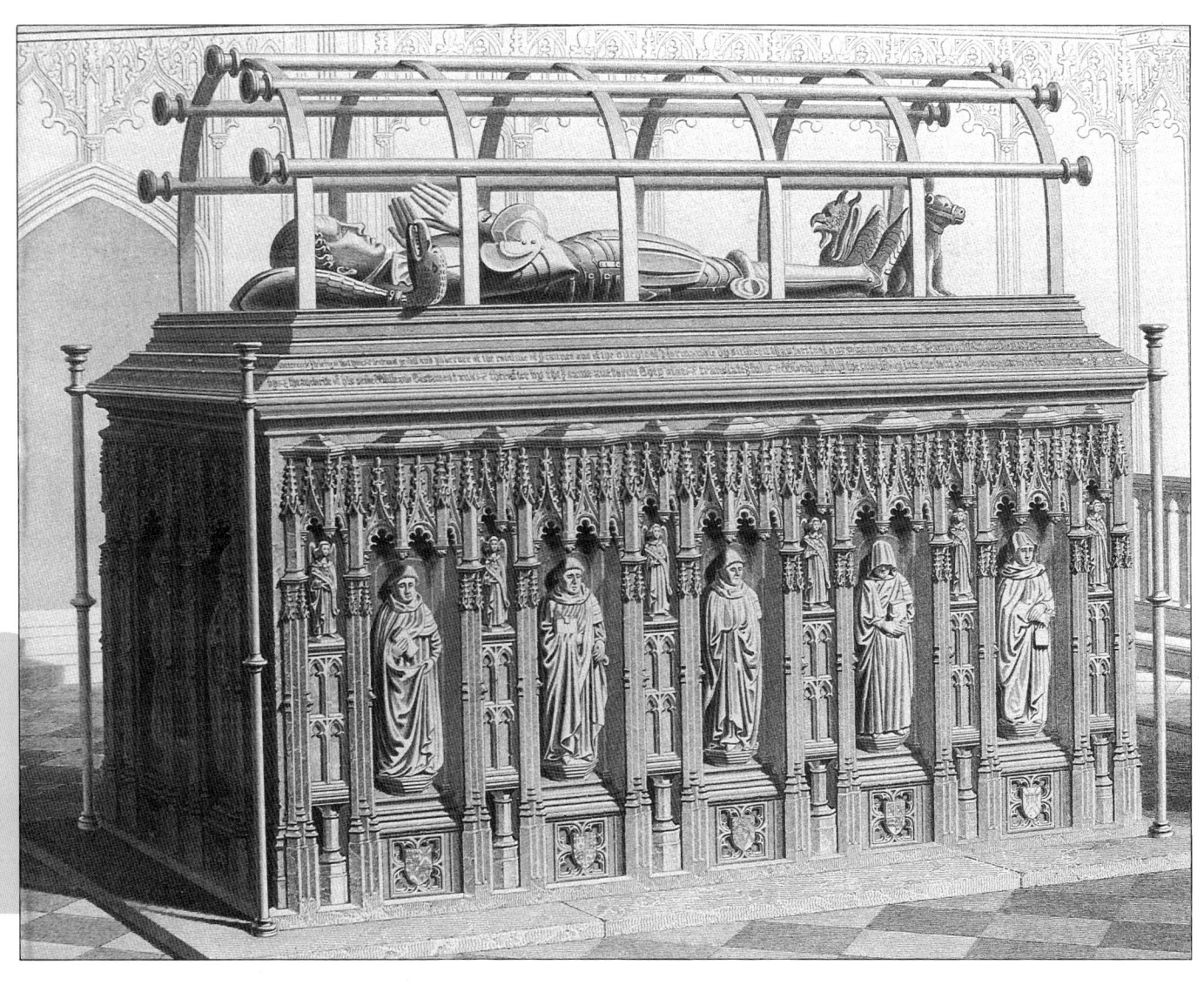

UNIT FIVE
LIFE IN A CASTLE

1. Elizabeth's home was her castle

Picture 5A shows Berkeley Castle, as it looks today.

Members of the Berkeley family have lived in this castle for hundreds of years. 600 years ago it was the home of Elizabeth Berkeley, who became the wife of Richard Beauchamp.

The castle was built so that the Berkeley family would be safe in times of danger. Which parts of the castle would help keep out enemies and robbers?

What does your home have which keeps it safe?

Which clues in this picture remind you that Berkeley Castle was a home, as well as a safe place?

5A

Picture 5B is a plan of Berkeley Castle, as it looked when Elizabeth Berkeley lived there.

Using words from the plan, copy and complete these sentences about the castle:

1. The castle bedrooms were called _____.

2. Daily prayers were said in the _____.

3. Food was stored in the _____ and cooked in the _____.

4. Meals were eaten and people entertained in the _____.

Now add some sentences of your own about other things the plan shows. Which buildings and rooms that were parts of Elizabeth's home THEN are not parts of most homes NOW? Which parts of homes NOW were not parts of Elizabeth's home THEN?

5B

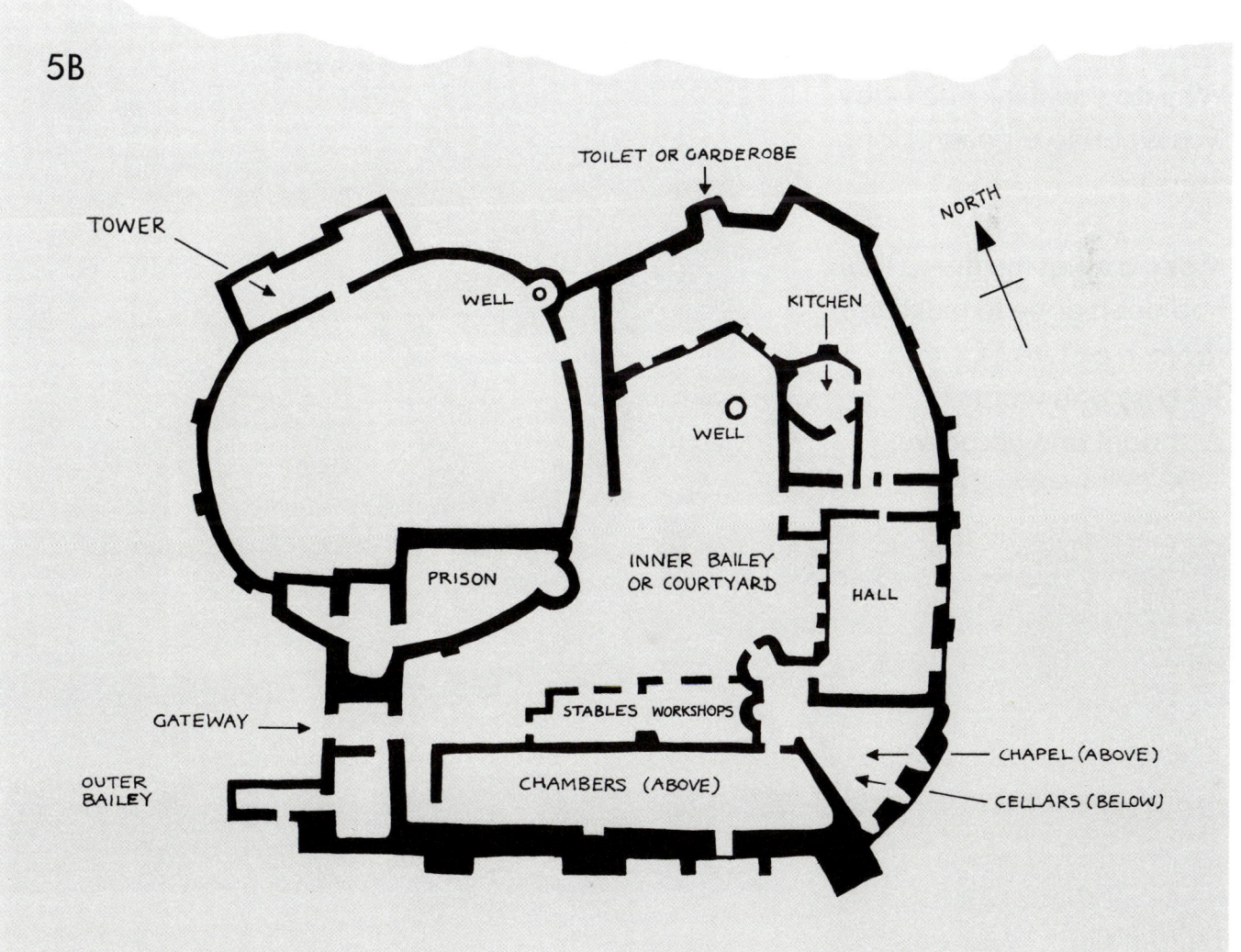

2. Home comforts

Picture 5C shows the kind of room in which Elizabeth Berkeley would have slept. Which person was the lady of the castle in this picture? Why were her servants called ladies-in-waiting?

Write a sentence to say what each lady-in-waiting was doing.

Then draw a picture of one of them.

Why do you think each lady was wearing a hat and long dress?

Make a list of the things that had been done to make the room in picture 5C:
1. cosy and warm.
2. bright and attractive.

5C

Rooms like the one in 5C were more pleasant and comfortable than most other places in a castle. Why were most parts of a castle often cold and dark?

Find out from books where the ordinary soldiers and servants who looked after Berkeley Castle would have slept.

Which parts of Berkeley Castle would have been smelly or dirty places to spend time?

Make a list of those things which make your home a comfortable place to live. Which modern "home comfort" do you think the people of Berkeley Castle would have enjoyed most?

3. At work in the castle

Many people worked in Berkeley Castle at the time Elizabeth Berkeley lived there. The pictures on these pages show different people doing their everyday jobs.

Write a sentence to say what each person was doing and another to say why each job was important.

Many of the surnames that we use today tell us about the jobs that people did in the past.

Think of a surname for each of the people in these pictures. Are there children in your school who have these surnames?

5D

5E

5F

5G

Now look back at pictures 5A and 5B. Use the plan of the castle to work out where the people in these pictures would have done their everyday jobs.

Imagine you were standing in the centre of the bailey or courtyard 600 years ago . . .

What things could you see being:
(a) made, (b) mended, (c) cleaned, (d) fed, (e) trained, (f) moved?
What things could you smell?
What sounds could you hear?

Draw a picture to show the castle at work in the days of Elizabeth Berkeley. Then write about the different things you have drawn.

5H

5I

4. Comings and goings

Every day many people went in and came out of a castle.

How did travellers enter or leave the castle in picture 5J?

Which person might have gone out of the castle:
1. to talk with her servants?
2. to take a letter to London?
3. to exercise his horse and dog?
4. to keep her Lady company?
5. to pick an onion from the herb garden?

These people visited Berkeley Castle when Elizabeth lived there.

5K
>   a doctor and nurse
>   Katherine Candelmaker
>   a group of actors
>   the parish priest
>   a goldsmith from London

Write a sentence to say why you think each visit was made.

5J

Many foods and other items had to be sent into a castle.

Look for the people at work in picture 5J. What was each person doing? Which items were sent into the castle because of this work?

What do you think happened to things castle people had used up or no longer wanted?

Imagine it was a summer's day in the year 1421.
You were on sentry duty at the entrance to Berkeley Castle.
Make a list of the people who came in and went out of the castle, how and why they were travelling and what they had with them.

5. From kitchen to hall

The kitchen was often a busy place in a castle.
When Earl Richard came to Berkeley in 1421, the kitchen staff had 200 people a day to feed.

5L shows kitchen servants at work.
Write about each job you see being done and draw the object each servant used to do it.

Choose words from this box to say what you think the kitchen and food in a castle were like.

sometimes	fresh	dirty
noisy	neat	never
untidy	quiet	cold
warm	clean	always

Write sentences to say why you chose the words you did.

5L

5M tells us what the Great Hall of a castle looked like.

Use the words in the box below to make lists about:

1. things you can see in the picture.
2. things you can see in a school dining room today.

servers	forks
supervisors	tablecloths
dogs	musicians
guests	a queue
long tables	

Add some words of your own to each list. Then underline those words which are in both lists.

People ate and drank these things in one day in Berkeley Castle.

5N

Large white loaves:	146
Red wine:	10½ gallons
Ale:	68 gallons
Herrings:	180
Oysters:	300

What things do the kitchen staff in your school order in large numbers?

5M

6. A day with Elizabeth

The pictures on these pages will help you imagine what a day in the life of Elizabeth Berkeley may have been like.

Use the pictures to write a sentence about each of the things she did.

Which part of the day did Elizabeth spend outside the castle?
Look once more at picture 5B.
Where might she have done the other things you have written about?

Use the word and picture clues in this unit to make a list of other things Elizabeth might have done during a day at Berkeley Castle.

Draw a picture to show her doing one of them.

5O

5P

5Q

5R

5S

5T

Which of the things she did would
Elizabeth have done:
1. on most days?
2. not very often?

How might what she did depend on:
1. the time of year?
2. who entered or left the castle?

Think of other reasons why she might
do different things at different times.

Which parts of Elizabeth's day would
you have:
1. enjoyed?
2. not enjoyed?
Say why in each case.

Make lists of:
1. the jobs your mum does.
2. the different things she
   does to relax.

How is her daily life
different from the life
Elizabeth Berkeley led?

7. To take you further

Fill each row of blank squares in the castle wall with the surname of a person who worked inside.

These clues will help you:

1. Made the ale.

2. Plucked a merry tune.

3. Looked after the horses.

4. Made the bread.

5. Was skilled with bow and arrow.

6. Made clothes for her Lady.

7. Was learning to be a knight.

8. Gave colour to cloth.

9. Prepared the meals.

10. Moved goods from place to place.

11. Worked with stone.

12. Mended the stable roof.

13. Kept the accounts.

14. Cut up the meat.

Make your own wall of castle words.
Write clues for your classmates to guess the words you chose.

No two castles were the same . . . . or were they?

Which of these things is true for:
1. castle A?
2. castle B?
3. both castles?

Use the pictures to add more ideas to the lists you have begun.

1. People lived there.
2. Still lived in.
3. Now in ruins.
4. Has battlements on walls.
5. Crossed drawbridge to enter.
6. Chimneys on the roof.

Castle A

Castle B

Explore a castle yourself! Which of these clues to everyday life can you find?

Make sketches of them.

How different is your castle from Berkeley Castle?

Kitchen		Staircase		Window	
Oven	✓	Chimney		Guardroom	
Hall		Sink		Toilet	
Well		Storeroom		Courtyard	
Chamber		Fireplace		Chapel	

UNIT SIX
CHANGES IN TRAVEL

1. Elizabeth goes to London

Today many families own a car.
But 600 years ago there were no cars.
Travelling was difficult and dangerous.
The roads were often hard and bumpy, or wet and muddy, and robbers might attack anyone who passed by.

Few people travelled far from where they were born.
Those who did travel usually walked from place to place.
Others rode horses.
Elizabeth Berkeley sometimes rode in a carriage, like the one in picture 6A.
This unit is about the changes in private road travel, from the days when the horse and carriage were used to the age of the motor car.

6A

In the spring of 1421, Elizabeth Berkeley left Berkeley Castle (near Bristol) to travel by carriage to London.

Her daughters, servants and some soldiers travelled with her.

The journey of about 200 kilometres took two weeks to complete.

Why might Elizabeth's journey have taken so long? Why did such a large group of people travel with her? Do you think that taking a carriage was the best way for Elizabeth to travel?

Look in an atlas. How would road travellers make the journey from Bristol to London today? Would the journey take a few minutes, hours, days or weeks?

2. The coming of the car

Journeys were still being made by horse and carriage 100 years ago.
Doctor William Curtis owned a carriage like the one in picture 6B.
He used it to visit his patients.

Look at 6A and 6B to see how different his carriage was from the one used
by Elizabeth Berkeley.

Which of these things did the doctor's carriage have?
Which did Elizabeth's carriage have?
Make two lists.
Then add more items to each list.
Are there things in both lists?

springs for comfort
canvas top
wooden framework
no seat for driver
glass windows

6B

6C

15757

Now look at the machine in 6C.
It was built 100 years ago by a
German called Daimler.
Daimler's machine did not need
a horse to pull it.
It had an engine that was driven
by petrol.

Was Daimler's car a better way
to travel than the horse and
carriage of Doctor Curtis?

Copy and complete this chart to
help you decide.
Tick one box in each row. 1 has
been done for you.

	6B	6C
1. Could travel faster	✓	
2. Protected in bad weather		
3. Could seat more passengers		
4. Less chance of breakdown		
5. Easier to steer		
6. Less costly to run		

3. The car and the law

At first, few cars were seen on the roads of Britain. This was because it was against the law to drive at more than 4 miles (about 6½ kilometres) an hour. Also, a man had to walk in front of each car, waving a red flag.
Can you think why?
Why did those people who had bought cars not like this law?

Look for the owner of the car in picture 6D.
How can you tell that he was a rich man?
Why do you think he had bought a car, when it could only travel so slowly?

6D

Now draw a picture of the man carrying the flag in 6D. Add some sentences below your picture to say:

1. why his job was such a boring one.
2. how his arms and feet felt at the end of the day.
3. what people shouted or threw at him, as the car passed by.

Do you think this man would have liked or disliked the red flag law?

In 1896 the law was changed.

Cars could then travel at 12 miles (19 kilometres) per hour.

Find out how fast cars are allowed to travel today:

1. in the centre of towns.
2. on motorways.

4. Happy motoring?

Picture 6E and the words in this box will help you imagine what a journey by car was like in the year 1902.

The car in 6E was stronger and could go faster than those in 6C and 6D.

But cars were still uncomfortable to travel in and would often break down.

Use the picture and word clues on these pages to work out:

1. what the people in the front and back of the car were wearing.
2. why they were wearing these things.
3. what things might have gone wrong with a car on the road.

accident	child
sheep	smoke
excited	amused
engine	fast
wet	cold
farmer	policeman
brakes	bumpy
frightened	petrol
dusty	angry
tyres	noisy

6E

Which words in the box might tell you what the carriage driver and his passengers in 6E were thinking as the car passed by? Why might they have felt like this? What do you imagine the young girl and old man in picture 6D were thinking about the car they saw?

Now write some sentences about a car journey you made on an October's day in 1902.

Write about: the car, the road, the people travelling with you, the people and animals you passed by.

The picture and word box should give you ideas.

5. Cars for everyone

The first cars were made one at a time by skilful craftsmen.
Because of this only rich people had the money to buy them. But an American named Ford found a way of making cars more quickly and cheaply than before.

Copy and complete the sentence below to
say how it was done. Use these words to
do this:

one	same	different	many	each

_____ parts were added to _____ car, as a line of cars moved around Ford's factory.
A worker added the _____ part to each car that passed him. In this way
_____ cars could be made in _____ factory at once.

What does picture 6F show happening?

6F

Picture 6G shows James Howe and his family in the car he was able to buy after the First World War.

This list shows how James used his car.

1. Go to work
2. Take child to school
3. Go shopping
4. Go on holiday
5. Visit relatives
6. Picnic in countryside

Why might he have never done 2, 4 and 6 before he had a car?
How do you think he did 1, 3 and 5 at that time?

Write some sentences about where you think the family were going in the picture. Draw a picture or diagram to show the different ways a family might use their car today.

6G

6. The Walkers visit Wales

This year the Walker family went on holiday in their car.
Daniel and Lisa talked about the things they saw on the way to the coast.

Can you match each speech box with one of these pictures?

To get there quicker we can use the motorway . . .

Traffic jams are a big problem in busy places where the roads are not so wide . . .

Thousands of people must work at making, selling or repairing cars, and the parts for them . . .

Accidents can happen when people drive too fast or without care . . .

There's a place for you to park, dad . . .

We'll need lots of petrol for such a long journey . . .

6K

The pictures show many of the changes the car has made to the world around us.

Make a list of the changes you can see on these pages.

Then talk with your teacher and class mates about which of the changes were good things

and which were bad ones ☒

6L

Write a sentence about each change to say why it was good or bad.

How has the car changed the area where you live?

1. Ask older people to talk about the time when few cars were on the road.
2. Make drawings of CLUES TO THE CAR you can find, such as garages and parking meters.

6M

7. To take you further

The pictures below show some of the important "steps forward" from carriage to car.
Write about:
1. what the changes were.
2. why each change was important.
Use these words in your answers:

comfortable   faster   safer

Then match each of these changes with one of the vehicles shown in this unit. This should help you put the changes in the order in which they happened.

Collect pictures or make drawings of old carriages and motor cars.
Look for new ideas in the way each was made to help you put them in order of age.

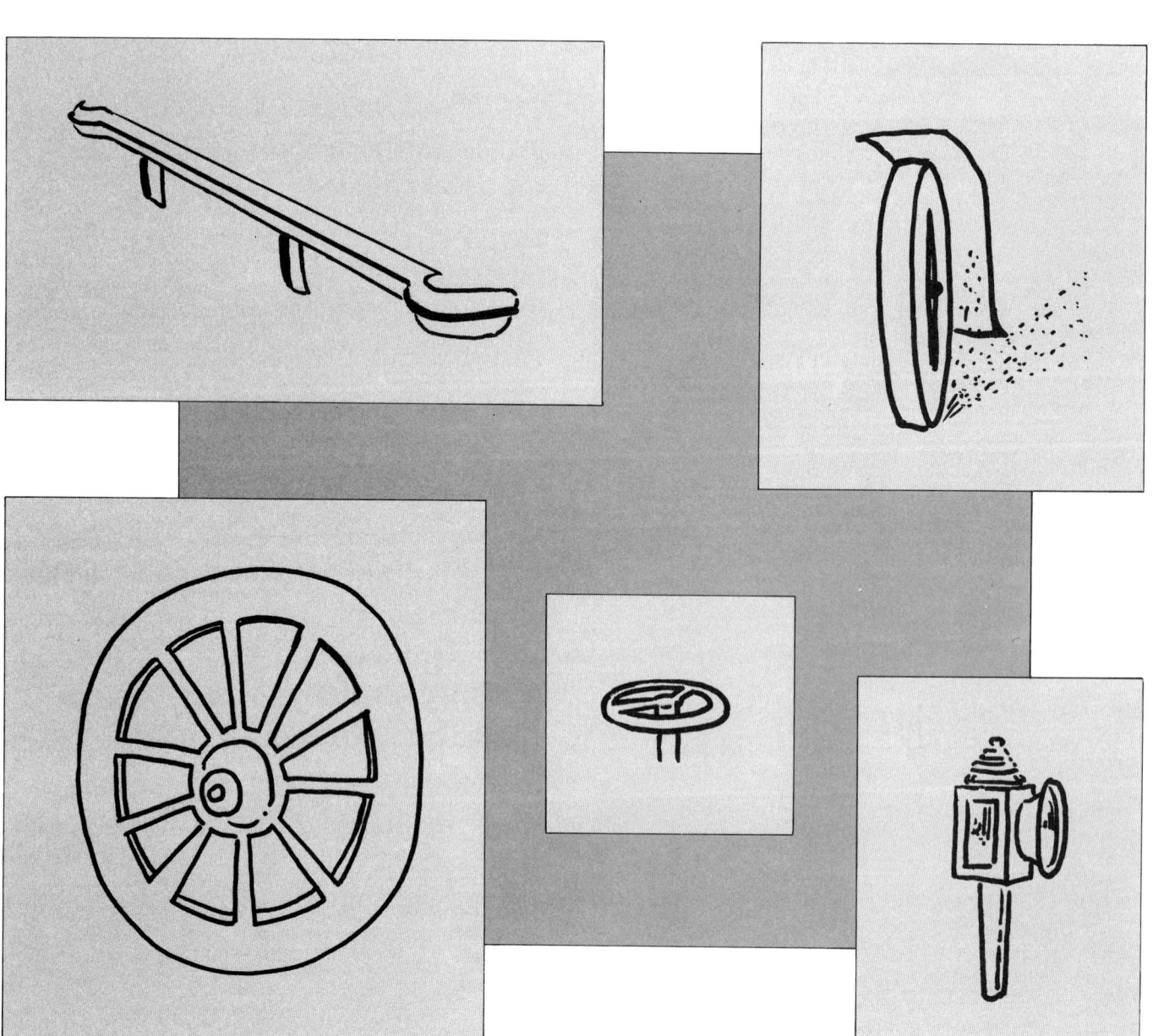

Some children who live in Cluebury have been counting the vehicles that pass their school.

They counted between 9:30 a.m. and 10 a.m., and then drew this graph:

	5	10	15	20	25	30	35	40	45	50	55	60	65	70	75	80	85	90	95	100
CARS	■	■	■	■	■	■	■	■	■	■	■	■	■	■	■	■	■	■		
VANS AND LORRIES	■	■	■	■	■	■	■													
BUSES	■	■																		
BICYCLES	■																			
MOTOR BIKES AND CYCLES	■	■																		
HORSE AND CART																				

How many motor vehicles passed Cluebury school during this half-hour?

Find out how many pass your own school during the same time and draw a graph like this one.

Can you imagine what Cluebury looked like 100 years ago?
Pictures 3A and 3N will help you think.

What if some Victorian schoolchildren had done the same counting exercise?
Write down:
1. which rows of figures would have gone up.
2. which would have gone down.
3. why these things would have happened.

Henry the Fourth
1399—1413

Edward the Seventh   1901—1910

Victoria   1837—1901

George the Sixth   1936—1952

Henry the Sixth   1422—1461

These pictures are on display in Cluebury Art Gallery.

They show the rulers of England when Richard Beauchamp was alive and when James Howe was alive.

The dates tell you the number of years or period of time when each ruler was on the throne.

Can you place these rulers in the order in which they ruled?
Start with the earliest in time.

Edward the Eighth also ruled when James Howe was alive, but was never crowned king.
Find out where Edward should come in this order.

Richard the Second
1377–1399

Henry the Fifth   1413–1422

George the Fifth   1910–1936

Next, copy and complete these sentences about the rulers:

1. _____ and _____ ruled for the shortest periods of time.
2. Queen Victoria ruled for the _____ period.
3. James Howe died during the time when _____ ruled.
4. Richard Beauchamp was born during _____.
5. Edward the Seventh ruled _____ George the Fifth.
6. _____ after Henry the Sixth.

Now write about these events from this book.

Link each event with a ruler and time word from these pages:

1. Thomas Curtis drowned at sea (see page 22).
2. James Howe married (page 48).
3. Elizabeth Beauchamp travelled to London (page 79).
4. The First World War took place (page 6).
5. Daimler's motor carriage was invented (page 81).
6. Richard Beauchamp's tomb was completed (pages 60 and 63).

How We Know

There are a number of different sorts of clues to help you relive the past. There are spoken clues like 1A when Grandma Walker told Daniel about her father. There are picture clues: drawings, photographs or paintings like 2I which shows how a rich Victorian family spent an evening at home.

There are object clues which may be small like the shrapnel in 1E or as large as Berkeley Castle.

There are written clues like 3E which is a list of names from a street directory.

Into which of these groups would you place these clues: 1C, 1F, 2G, 3J, 5J?

1A

Your great-grandad was a soldier during the First World War. This photo was taken soon after he joined the army. He found this German helmet on the ground after a battle. This postcard told us he had been injured fighting in France. A piece of shrapnel like this was removed from your great-grandad's leg. This photo shows him in hospital in England. He was given this medal at the end of the war.

3E

```
273  Winn Benjamin, milliner
275  Scott Joseph E., woollen manfr.
277  Horsfall Mrs.
279  Dickinson Anthony
281  Madden Wm. A., inland rev. officer
```

1E

5A

Now copy and complete this chart about the clues in this book. Find examples from each unit which are not mentioned on page 94 to do this.

CLUES	Page
An object clue which tells you about people and events in the trenches	
A written clue which tells you about everyday life in a Victorian family	
Two picture clues to show how a street has changed through time	
An object clue which tells you about the life of Richard Beauchamp	
A written clue about day-to-day life in a castle	
Three picture clues to show how the motor car has developed	

21

From Page 59: The English decided to starve the people of Rouen into surrender.

Thomas Nelson and Sons Ltd
Nelson House   Mayfield Road
Walton-on-Thames   Surrey
KT12 5PL   UK

51 York Place
Edinburgh
EH1 3JD   UK

Thomas Nelson (Hong Kong) Ltd
Toppan Building 10/F
22A Westlands Road
Quarry Bay   Hong Kong

Distributed in Australia by

Thomas Nelson Australia
480 La Trobe Street
Melbourne   Victoria 3000
and in Sydney, Brisbane, Adelaide and Perth

First published by Thomas Nelson and Sons Ltd 1988
ISBN   0-17-426017-2
NPN   987654321

Printed and Bound in United Kingdom

Credits for photographs used in this volume are due to the following:

Adams Picture Library: pp. 77, 88; Art Directors Photo Library: pp. 4, 88, 89; BBC Hulton Picture Library: pp. 8, 20, 42, 43, 66–7, 75, 78–9, 81, 92; Beamish North of England Open Air Museum: pp. 26–7; Bridgeman Art Library: pp. 69, 92; British Library: pp. 12, 50, 51, 52–3, 54–5, 56–7, 58–9, 60, 61, 68, 69, 70–71, 72, 74, 75, 92; Camera Press: p. 9; Sheena Callender: pp. 1, 8; Central Office of Information: p. 19; A.E.W. Dacre: p. 38; Keith Dickson: p. 87; Mary Evans Picture Library: pp. 31, 73, 75; Ford Motor Company: p. 86; John R Freeman: pp. 4, 30; Hampshire County Museum Services: pp. 21, 22; Illustrated London News: pp. 10–11; Imperial War Museum: pp. 8, 9, 14, 15, 16–17; Institute of Agricultural History and Museum of English Rural Life: pp. 26–27; Roshini Kempadoo/Format: pp. 24–25, 32, 35, 36, 39; Leeds City Library: pp. 20, 34, 37; Leighton House Museum and Art Gallery: pp. 28–9; Mansell Collection: pp. 23, 33, 43, 84–5; Museum of London: pp. 42, 62; National Army Museum: p. 13; National Motor Museum: pp. 82–3; National Portrait Gallery: pp. 92, 93; National Trust: p. 77; Thomas Nelson & Sons: p. 6; Chris Ridgers Photography: pp. 6, 7, 26–7, 88; Science Museum: p. 80; Skyscan: p. 78; Tate Gallery: pp. 44–5; Warwickshire County Council: p. 63; York Castle Museum: pp. 7, 18;

We are grateful to the Abbey House Museum, the Bradford Industrial Museum, and the Gunnersbury Park Museum for their permissions and help with the photography on pp. 32, 24–5 and 26–7 respectively.

Special thanks are due to Jim Lawson at the Beamish North of England Open Air Museum, Mrs Heap at the Leeds City Library Local History Department, Richard Stansfield at York Castle Museum and the Media Services of the British Library.

Illustrations: Chris Hahner p. 47; Steve Jones pp. 48–9; David Mitcheson p. 46
Cover Photographs: Popper Foto/Zefa Picture Library